Paul

A missionary for Jesus

By Tim Sawyer

Paul: A missionary for Jesus

Copyright © 2017, 2018 by Sawyer Publications
All rights reserved. No part of this book may be reproduced in any form without permission in writing from the author. Reviewers may quote brief passages in reviews.

Disclaimer and FTC Notice

No part of this publication may be reproduced or transmitted in any form or by any means, mechanical or electronic, including photocopying or recording, or by any information storage and retrieval system, or transmitted by email without permission in writing from the publisher.

While all attempts have been made to verify the information provided in this publication, neither the author nor the publisher assumes any responsibility for errors, omissions, or contrary interpretations of the subject matter herein.

Neither the author nor the publisher assumes any responsibility or liability whatsoever on behalf of the purchaser or reader of these materials. Any perceived slight of any individual or organization is purely unintentional.

All Scripture quotations, unless otherwise indicated, are taken from the Holy Bible, New International Version®, NIV®. Copyright ©1973, 1978, 1984, 2011 by Biblica, Inc.™ Used by permission of Zondervan. All rights reserved worldwide. www.zondervan.com The "NIV" and "New International Version" are trademarks registered in the United States Patent and Trademark Office by Biblica, Inc.™

Table of Contents

Introduction 5

Week One – Early Life 7

Week Two – New Believer 23

Week Three – New Missionary......................... 39

Week Four – First Journey 55

Week Five – Second Journey 71

Week Six – Third Journey 87

Week Seven – Final Years............................... 103

Leader's Guide 121

Acknowledgments 127

Dedicated to Sherwood Sawyer

Introduction

Paul the Apostle, also known as Saul of Tarsus, was an amazing missionary in the early church. At first, Saul arrested Christians. Then he became a Christian as well as a missionary who tried to persuade others to become Christians too!

This book presents Paul's story in 50 daily parts. You can read it all at once or study it one day at a time. Much of the content comes from the New Testament book of Acts in the Bible. The author weaves in historical facts and geographical details.

The purpose of this book is to help you deepen your relationship with God. Open your mind to what God is saying. Let the Bible impact you.

The advantage of doing an individual Bible study is that you can deal with private issues.

The advantage of doing a group Bible study is that you progress more quickly in your walk of faith.

Group discussions help you grow. They bring out new ideas that you may not think of by yourself.

God uses those around you to encourage you and to help you with changes you may wish to make. You may be the person God uses to help others.

Week One – Early Life

Day 1: Born into tribe of Benjamin

Day 2: Studied under Gamaliel

Day 3: Supported Stephen's death

Day 4: Persecuted the church

Day 5: Planned a trip to Damascus

Day 6: Met Jesus on the Road

Day 7: Encountered Ananias

Day 1: Born into tribe of Benjamin

Saul was born into a Hebrew family about the year AD 5 in Tarsus. Rome ruled this port city. His father probably was a tent maker or merchant.

Saul was taught to follow the Jewish faith at an early age. His father was a Pharisee. This sect of Judaism had many strict lifestyle rules to obey.

Saul demonstrated a natural aptitude for learning. His family came from the tribe of Benjamin with its heritage of King Saul and Mordecai the Jew.

Saul grew up along the banks of the Cydnus River. Melting snow from the Taurus Mountains flowed past Tarsus down to the Mediterranean Sea.

The city of Tarsus, in the region of Cilicia, lies in southeastern Turkey. Saul's father had him leave home to attend rabbinical school in Jerusalem.

Saul said goodbye to the valley of his homeland. He boarded a southbound ship. Cyprus Island was on his right. Mount Lebanon was on his left. He finally arrived at the rebuilt harbor of Caesarea.

He was about ten years old when he completed the 400-mile journey. Imagine his amazement when he climbed the hill and first saw Jerusalem.

Bible verse:

In Philippians 3:5, Paul wrote that he was "circumcised on the eighth day, of the people of Israel, of the tribe of Benjamin, a Hebrew of Hebrews; in regard to the law, a Pharisee."

Discussion question:

What was your religious heritage as a child?

Day 2: Studied under Gamaliel

Jewish travelers passing through Tarsus would tell Saul stories of the Holy Land. Now he could see the realities for himself. His sister married and moved to Jerusalem. Possibly Saul lived with his sister while attending school.

Several hundred boys were in Jerusalem to attend rabbinical school. Saul studied at the one founded by Hillel. After him, his son Simeon led the school until about the time Jesus was born. Simeon passed the leadership mantle down to his son Gamaliel.

Maybe at this time, Saul befriended a Levite boy from Cyprus named Joseph. They hadn't grown up in Israel. They were Hellenistic Jews (from Greek-speaking areas). Joseph would be called Barnabas.

Gamaliel taught his students to be skilled in oral arguments. Saul learned to value honest judgment, to study Greek authors, and to love the Jewish law.

He completed his schooling about the year AD 20. After that, Saul returned home to Tarsus. He must have learned the tentmaking business as a young man. In his spare time, he studied Greek literature and the Scriptures. Saul was not in Jerusalem nor Israel during the ministry years of Jesus.

Bible verse:

Paul said in Acts 22:3, "I am a Jew, born in Tarsus of Cilicia, but brought up in this city. I studied under Gamaliel and was thoroughly trained in the law of our ancestors. I was just as zealous for God as any of you are today."

Discussion question:

Think of a school teacher who influenced you. What impact did that teacher have on your life?

Day 3: Supported Stephen's death

Saul heard stories in the synagogue at Tarsus of those who believed in one called Jesus. Saul never saw Jesus in the flesh, but what he heard disturbed him. So he returned to Jerusalem by AD 32.

Many knew him from his time with Gamaliel. Saul knew the Scriptures. He possessed an ability to think on his feet, and he excelled in oral debates.

Now the energetic young Saul sought to defend the Jewish faith. When he and his friends encountered Stephen, they were unable to resist his arguments. They made up accusations and arrested Stephen.

Stephen gave a compelling defense of his faith by using the Law of Moses that Saul himself loved. Stephen proclaimed that everyone knew that he spoke the truth. His speech reminded people of an old prophet. The Sanhedrin could not ignore him.

While they might not have the legal authority to put Stephen to death, they had the power to do it. Maybe the king or governor was out of town at that moment. In any case, Saul approved of their plan. Those who stoned Stephen laid their outer garments at Saul's feet. When Stephen saw Jesus, he asked the Lord to forgive those who killed him.

Bible verse:

Regarding the death of Stephen we read in Acts 8:1: "And Saul approved of their killing him."

Discussion question:

If you were Saul, how might the death of Stephen impact your future?

Day 4: Persecuted the church

Throughout the next couple years, Saul tried hard to destroy the church. He continually hunted down Jesus followers. At first, his focus was the city of Jerusalem and the surrounding towns. Then he expanded his efforts throughout all of Israel.

Saul acted like an officer who was extremely angry at the criminals that he arrested. Saul pursued all who followed Jesus because such believers were perverting his faith. They were enemies of God who had forfeited their right to live in peace.

He threatened violence on the men, on the women, and on their families. Children could be removed from their home if their parents did not recant their faith in Jesus. The adults were arrested, flogged, tortured, or killed. All believers feared Saul.

Saul considered himself blameless before God. The Jewish leaders funded his activities. While the original apostles were left alone, their converts were in grave danger. Most fled Jerusalem.

Those like Philip and his four unmarried daughters traveled throughout Israel proclaiming the Lord and preaching the gospel. Many came to faith.

Bible verse:

Acts 8:3 says, "Saul began to destroy the church. Going from house to house, he dragged off both men and women and put them in prison."

Discussion question:

What might be the most challenging thing about going to prison for what you believe?

Day 5: Planned a trip to Damascus

Saul continued his time of threatening those who followed the Way taught by Jesus. In AD 34, he planned to travel to Damascus, one of the oldest cities in the world. The city had a sizeable Jewish population. Saul likely had reason to expect that he might find more believers there.

One may assume that Saul had already been to cities closer to Jerusalem during the prior year. The Jesus followers had had to travel further away from Jerusalem to avoid persecution.

After Saul cleaned out Jerusalem, his sights shifted to the surrounding communities of Judea. Later his efforts would be expanded into Samaria where Philip had preached.

Believers became witnesses for Jesus in Jerusalem, Judea, Samaria, and the known world. Saul hunted them down. Maybe he passed through Nazareth in Galilee and walked the roads that Jesus walked. But Saul looked to go beyond the Sea of Galilee.

Saul moved out of Israel. From the Golan Heights, he might look ahead to the distant plateau and see the city of Damascus, Syria. Saul obtained letters of authority to arrest any believers he found.

Bible verse:

Saul approached the high priest, and in Acts 9:2 Saul "asked him for letters to the synagogues in Damascus, so that if he found any there who belonged to the Way, whether men or women, he might take them as prisoners to Jerusalem."

Discussion question:

Why do you think people referred to the early Christians as "the Way"?

Day 6: Met Jesus on the Road

From the Golan Heights Saul could look left across the Hula Valley to Mount Hermon. Damascus lay ahead 25 miles north. Saul the Pharisee marched onward seeking Christians to arrest.

Saul approached the city around midday. Soon he expected to see its taller buildings in the distance. Suddenly all Saul could see was a bright light. And then he fell to the ground and saw nothing at all!

A voice called Saul by name and spoke to him in Hebrew, "Saul, why are you persecuting me? Doing this is dangerous. It leads to trouble."

Saul asked, "Who are you, Lord?" He said, "I am Jesus of Nazareth, whom you are persecuting."

Stunned and overwhelmed by what just happened, Saul asked, "What do you want me to do?"

Jesus answered, "I have plans for you. Get up. Go into the city, and you will be told what to do."

Saul could see nothing. His companions had heard the voice, but they did not understand it. Saul said that he needed to go to Straight Street in Damascus to the home of Judas. His companions led him by the hand into the city and found that house.

Bible verse:

Saul responded in Acts 9:5: "Who are you, Lord?"

Discussion question:

What impact might a direct encounter with Jesus have on the future course of your life?

Day 7: Encountered Ananias

While at the house of Judas, Saul prayed for three days. He ate nothing. He drank nothing. His eyes were blind, but his mind could see that he needed to change. Saul understood that his life's passion to punish Christians was not what God wanted.

Meanwhile, the Lord appeared in a vision to Ananias, a devout Christian in Damascus. He arrived at the house of Judas on the third day.

Ananias asked for Saul of Tarsus. They took him to a room where he found a frail figure sitting on the floor and praying with his eyes closed.

He walked over beside the man and said, "Brother Saul." The man raised his face toward the sound. Ananias placed his hands on him and then he said, "Receive your sight and be filled with the Holy Spirit." Scales fell from his eyes, and he could see.

Then Ananias added, "God has called you to be a witness to the Gentiles. Rise and be baptized."

Saul stayed several days with the other believers in Damascus. Soon Saul went to the synagogues in the area and preached that Jesus was the Son of God. Everyone was amazed at his conversion.

Bible verse:

Acts 9:17 tells what happened when the two men met: "Ananias went to the house and entered it. Placing his hands on Saul, he said, 'Brother Saul, the Lord—Jesus, who appeared to you on the road as you were coming here—has sent me so that you may see again and be filled with the Holy Spirit.'"

Discussion question:

What do you think it means for a person to be filled with the Holy Spirit?

Prayer Concerns

Week Two – New Believer

Day 8: Traveled off to Arabia

Day 9: Began preaching Jesus

Day 10: Forced to flee Damascus

Day 11: Saw disciples in Jerusalem

Day 12: Stayed 15 days with Peter

Day 13: Sent back home to Tarsus

Day 14: Barnabas came for Saul

Day 8: Traveled off to Arabia

The Jews felt betrayed by Saul. They were furious. It might take them a little time, but eventually, the Jews would authorize someone to arrest him.

Since his conversion and commission had come directly from Jesus, Saul did not feel the need to immediately return to Jerusalem to consult with Peter, James, or the other apostles. He was a target. Anyone Saul was near would be in great danger.

Saul needed to get away. After he considered his options, he chose to leave the populated city and head for the desert rough areas. Roman and Greek writers referred to such places as "Arabia."

He probably teamed up with nomad herdsman, like those outside Tarsus or Damascus or the ancient city of Palmyra in Syria to the east. They lived in tents made from the hides of their sheep. The odor of killing sheep required them to avoid towns.

Since Saul could support himself as a tent maker, he related well to these traveling herdsmen. When he wasn't making tents, Saul preached the gospel to them and spent time with God. During these years of preparation, his spiritual faith in Jesus matured. Saul stayed away from AD 34 to AD 37.

Bible verse:

In Galatians 1:17 Paul tells us, "I did not go up to Jerusalem to see those who were apostles before I was, but I went into Arabia. Later I returned to Damascus."

Discussion question:

How can the experience of getting away to a camp or a retreat improve your spiritual life?

Day 9: Began preaching Jesus

After three years, Saul returned to Damascus. By then he was eager to embark on that divine mission which Jesus gave through the words of Ananias.

The believers in Damascus were encouraged by his return, but they knew that his presence increased their danger of possible persecution.

Saul had been trained in the Scriptures and in publicly debating theology in the synagogues. Now he was ready to speak for Jesus.

Everyone was amazed that Saul had switched sides. His conversion had an impact on both those who followed Jesus and those who didn't.

Saul used his experience and skill to attack beliefs he had formerly defended. He preached that Jesus was the Messiah who fulfilled the Scriptures.

Jews who lived too far from Jerusalem to attend the temple built local synagogues in which to worship God. First, they read the Scriptures. Then, someone would be invited to explain the Scripture or share a message from God. Synagogue worship gave Jewish Christians the perfect opportunity to share their belief that Jesus was the Messiah.

Bible verse:

Acts 9:22 says that "Saul grew more and more powerful and baffled the Jews living in Damascus by proving that Jesus is the Messiah."

Discussion question:

If you were to name your favorite preachers, who might it be and what do you like about them?

Day 10: Forced to flee Damascus

Saul continued to proclaim Christ among the Jews even though his ultimate calling would be to the Gentiles. Whoever his hearers were in Arabia, they were doubtless small groups in remote places. Jesus had called him to the nations of the world.

Now Saul was back in Damascus preaching that Jesus is the Son of God in full view of the masses. They recognized him as the man who previously had arrested Christians in the Jerusalem area.

His arguments and expressions were compelling. No one could refute him. He spoke for several weeks until the Jews had had enough.

They conspired to capture and kill Saul because of the effectiveness of his preaching. Maybe he left the city from time to time to visit with his nomad friends. The Jews watched for him at the city gates to catch him if he tried to leave the city. Saul found out about it, so he hid until he could get away.

The believers in Damascus were careful to protect Saul. City walls consisted of connected buildings with no outer doors or windows at the lower levels. They let him down in a basket through an opening high up in the wall. He escaped around AD 37.

Bible verse:

According to Acts 9:25, "his followers took him by night and lowered him in a basket through an opening in the wall."

Discussion question:

Describe a time when you tried to protect another believer who faced adversity.

Day 11: Saw disciples in Jerusalem

Saul went south from Damascus. How different this journey was from his time on that same road with Jesus three years earlier.

No longer was Saul breathing out hatred for those who followed the Lord. During his time away he developed a deep love for Jews and Gentiles alike.

The return trip to Jerusalem took him several days. When Saul got there, most of the disciples were afraid of him. Barnabas came to the rescue.

Barnabas, whose Hebrew name was Joseph, grew up in Cyprus. He had converted to Christianity. He and Saul were Hellenistic Jews (Greek-speaking) rather than Aramaic Jews who grew up in Israel.

It seems entirely possible that the physically larger Barnabas knew the famous Saul of Tarsus from their school days in Jerusalem. The two men had a lot in common being far from home.

The disciples respected Barnabas. He brought Saul to them. They listened. Barnabas described Saul's conversion. His life had exhibited a radical change. This same man who used to persecute believers now preached confidently in the name of Jesus.

Bible verse:

Acts 9:27 "Barnabas took him and brought him to the apostles. He told them how Saul on his journey had seen the Lord and that the Lord had spoken to him, and how in Damascus he had preached fearlessly in the name of Jesus."

Discussion question:

What do you suppose Saul was thinking now that he was returning to Jerusalem as a Christian?

Day 12: Stayed 15 days with Peter

The Christians at Damascus must have told Saul about a bold Galilean fisherman named Peter who was the leader of the twelve apostles. Saul wanted to meet him and to get to know this fisher of men.

Barnabas was related, possibly a brother, to Mary the mother of John Mark. This was the same Mary who had a maid named Rhoda in her home.

They were all friends. Saul explained his strange commission that Jesus called him on the road to Damascus to be a witness to the Gentiles.

Cephas (also called Peter) welcomed Saul. Peter understood preaching to Jews outside of Israel, but at that time, reaching non-Jews was foreign to him. God would deal with Peter on that issue later.

Saul was not a quiet Christian who worshipped at home on his own. He proclaimed Jesus boldly in the temple. Saul did this daily for two weeks.

Some Jews only spoke Hebrew and Aramaic. Saul was a Hellenistic Jew. He could debate with Jews from the many Greek-speaking countries who came to Jerusalem on business or for religious reasons. They could not refute Saul's teaching.

Bible verse:

Galatians 1:18, "Then after three years, I went up to Jerusalem to get acquainted with Cephas and stayed with him fifteen days."

Discussion question:

Why do you think Saul was eager to meet Peter?

Day 13: Sent back home to Tarsus

One day when Saul was praying in the temple, he fell into a trance and received a secret revelation. Jesus told him that the Jews would not accept his message. He must hurry and get out of Jerusalem.

Saul tried to explain to the Lord why the people in Jerusalem would listen to him. But Jesus said he was sending Saul far away to reach the Gentiles.

The Hellenistic Jews had had more than enough of Saul. They plotted to have him killed in Jerusalem, but word leaked out. He put them all in danger.

When the believers discovered this, they got Saul out of town. They brought him down to the port of Caesarea. From there he was shipped back home.

Saul would have to deal with issues involving the Roman Empire. Tiberius Caesar had been emperor from the time Saul studied under Gamaliel through the ministry of Jesus and for several years beyond.

Tiberius died in AD 37. Caligula became the new emperor. He preferred the pleasure perks of power.

Saul returned home as a believer by AD 38. Then he helped develop the church in Tarsus. Some of Saul's family members were already believers.

Bible verse:

Acts 9:30, "When the believers learned of this, they took him down to Caesarea and sent him off to Tarsus."

Discussion question:

If you were Saul, why might you be tempted to argue with God about the direction of your life?

Day 14: Barnabas came for Saul

Saul returned home to Tarsus. Possibly his parents were still alive. We can assume that he worked in the family business which involved making tents or selling tents in the market.

The last time Saul was in Tarsus, he was a Jew and a Pharisee. The Gentiles had been outcasts to him. Now he was a Christian and an apostle to Gentiles.

Saul preached Jesus in the synagogue. He prepared for his ministry to the Gentiles by reading Greek writers whose works were available in the library.

Eight years passed. During this time many Gentiles believed in Jesus. Their presence raised new issues for the young church which was mostly Jewish.

Peter visited Gentile believers that were close to Jerusalem. When they heard Gentiles were coming to Christ in Antioch, they wanted to check that out.

Some of the gospel preachers in Antioch had come from Cyprus where Barnabas grew up. The church at Jerusalem sent Barnabas to investigate.

When Barnabas saw the situation in Antioch, he wanted help. Then he remembered Saul. Barnabas went to Tarsus to find Saul about AD 46.

Bible verse:

Acts 11:25, "Then Barnabas went to Tarsus to look for Saul."

Discussion question:

If you needed help in a ministry, how might you go about finding someone to help you?

Prayer Concerns

Week Three – New Missionary

Day 15: Brought Saul to Antioch

Day 16: Brought aid to Jerusalem

Day 17: Returned with John Mark

Day 18: Separated as a missionary

Day 19: Began missionary journey

Day 20: Known as Paul on Paphos

Day 21: Abandoned by John Mark

Day 15: Brought Saul to Antioch

Saul heard the stories from Jerusalem travelers that Gentiles had been coming to Jesus for the past two years. Maybe he started churches in Cilicia.

Suddenly, his old friend Barnabas appeared on the streets of Tarsus. Saul was surprised and intrigued by the offer to come to Antioch. He sensed that the Holy Spirit had worked in his friend. After making the necessary arrangements, they left for Antioch. The trip took them around the northeast corner of the Mediterranean Sea. The journey was 100 miles or so depending on if they went by land or sea.

Seleucus founded Antioch. It was the most famous of 16 cities named after his father. Today it is the site of the modern city of Antakya, Turkey which is located on the Orontes River leading to the sea.

Barnabas and Saul spent a whole year evangelizing and building up the church at Antioch until AD 47. People first called them "Christians" in that city.

"Christian" is a Roman form of a Greek word that would offend the Jews. "Christ" means "Messiah." The Jews preferred the term "followers of the sect of the Nazarenes" without any connection to the Jewish Messiah. But the name Christian stuck.

Bible verse:

Barnabas came to Saul in Acts 11:26, "and when he found him, he brought him to Antioch. So for a whole year Barnabas and Saul met with the church and taught great numbers of people. The disciples were called Christians first at Antioch."

Discussion question:

How might Saul feel to be teaching in a church that reached vast numbers of people in a year?

Day 16: Brought aid to Jerusalem

Antioch attracted wealthy visitors. They pursued immoral worldly passions in the baths of Caligula. They dedicated the suburb of Daphne with its bay tree groves to that female nymph who had been pursued by the god Apollo in Greek mythology.

We can assume many of these wealthy partygoers got saved under the ministry of Barnabas and Saul. Thus, people with money became new Christians.

The city boasted beautiful buildings, but some had been destroyed in recent earthquakes during the reigns of Emperor Caligula and then later under Emperor Claudius. Jerusalem faced major famine. The cost of food increased so much that some in the Jerusalem church began to starve.

A prophet named Agabus came from Jerusalem to Antioch. He prophesized that the famine would become worldwide. They needed to do something. Antioch believers could give to help those in need.

The outward focused church at Antioch decided to help the suffering believers in Jerusalem. This new church raised a relief fund to help the old church. People gave according to their means. Barnabas and Saul were to deliver the money personally.

Bible verse:

Acts 11:30, "This they did, sending their gift to the elders by Barnabas and Saul."

Discussion question:

Why do you think the church chose Barnabas and Saul to deliver the relief monies personally?

Day 17: Returned with John Mark

Barnabas and Saul made the journey to Jerusalem with the gift for the needy. They probably went by ship and traveled with merchants. This method was safer than carrying the money overland on foot.

The journey from Antioch to Jerusalem was 300 miles. They would follow the Orontes River to the port of Seleucia on the Mediterranean Sea.

This port of Seleucia was named after Seleucus II, the same man who founded Antioch and named it after his father Antiochus II. He named six cities after his mother Laodice II, calling those Laodicea.

It seems likely that Barnabas and Saul traveled by ship with merchants and cargo rather than walk for hundreds of miles through the countryside. They could board a vessel at Seleucia, sail past Tyre to Caesarea and travel another 50 miles to Jerusalem.

One can imagine the suffering congregation was overjoyed with the gift. Those desperate Jewish Christians were in no position to turn down help.

When they came back to Antioch, Barnabas and Saul brought young John Mark along with them. Mark's mother was a sister or cousin to Barnabas.

Bible verse:

Acts 12:25, "When Barnabas and Saul had finished their mission, they returned from Jerusalem, taking with them John, also called Mark."

Discussion question:

What do you think might be some advantages in doing ministry with family members?

Day 18: Separated as a missionary

People came to Antioch from southern Europe, northern Africa, and all around the Middle East. The church reflected the overall population.

The church pastoral leadership included prophets and teachers. Five individuals were listed by name: Barnabas, Simeon, Lucius, Manaen, and Saul.

Saul may have been last to arrive, but his teaching skill became evident to all. Barnabas gained the respect of all who knew him. Since Barnabas chose Saul, everyone thought of them as a team.

Jesus challenged his followers to reach the world. The Antioch congregation had family and friends from far away. Many of these loved ones had not heard about Jesus Christ. Who would tell them?

Barnabas was skilled in bringing people together to worship the Lord. Saul was skilled in teaching how Christianity was superior to other religions.

The church focused on solemn prayer and fasting desiring to spread the Gospel. Then the Holy Spirit separated Barnabas and Saul. Through the Spirit, the Lord called these two men to be missionaries. We expect they willingly supported this decision.

Bible verse:

Acts 13:2, "While they were worshiping the Lord and fasting, the Holy Spirit said, "Set apart for me Barnabas and Saul for the work to which I have called them."

Discussion question:

How do you suppose the church determined that it was the Holy Spirit who called Barnabas and Saul?

Day 19: Began missionary journey

The church held a consecration service for the two missionaries. Leaders laid their hands on them as a symbolic sign of agreement with the Holy Spirit.

Barnabas and Saul departed Antioch in late AD 47 or early AD 48. The pair made their way down the Orontes River to the port city of Seleucia. They sailed over to the Mediterranean island of Cyprus.

These missionaries were probably 40 years old or more. Mark served as an assistant and helped carry supplies. He was perhaps 20 years younger.

The destination of Cyprus may have been divinely indicated in some revelation to the Antioch church. Barnabas grew up on Cyprus. The eastern edge of the island was 80 miles from Seleucia. They might see Mount Olympus on Cyprus on a clear day.

They planned to reach the lost among the Gentiles, but they would find encouragement from believers already connected to those in the Antioch church.

They sailed beyond the tip of Cyprus to Salamis, to the north of Famagusta. The city was full of Jewish merchants trading fruit, wine, flax, and honey. The two preached the Word of God in synagogues.

Bible verse:

Acts 13:4, "The two of them, sent on their way by the Holy Spirit, went down to Seleucia and sailed from there to Cyprus."

Discussion question:

What do you suppose Saul thought about when he first left the Antioch Church to be a missionary?

Day 20: Known as Paul on Paphos

Barnabas may have been from Salamis, but they wanted to preach to the regions beyond. They sailed around the southern end of the island to the city of Paphos on the southwestern side.

Here they found a mixture of Greek culture and the type of amusements the Romans seemed to enjoy. The Roman governor Sergius Paulus asked to hear Barnabas and Saul tell him about the Word of God. The governor's interest peaked when they spoke of the kingdom of God through faith in Jesus Christ.

The governor, or proconsul, was sidetracked by his friend Elymas. He tried to keep Sergius Paulus from believing in Jesus. The Holy Spirit led Saul to confront the wicked friend boldly. Saul told Elymas that he would be temporarily struck blind. Then Elymas fell back and needed people to help him. Seeing this, the governor believed in Jesus.

Greek-speaking Jews had two names. Barnabas had stopped using his given Hebrew name, Joseph. Saul had not used his Greek named Paulos (Paul in English) until he led the proconsul Sergius Paulus to Christ. His name "Paulus" is the Roman version of Paul. From AD 48 on, Saul called himself Paul.

Bible verse:

Acts 13:9, "Then Saul, who was also called Paul, filled with the Holy Spirit..."

Discussion question:

How might you change your name or your speech when dealing with different people groups?

Day 21: Abandoned by John Mark

Paul, Barnabas, and Mark sailed from Paphos into the bay of Pamphylia to the inland town of Perga (near the modern city of Antalya). Perga was more than 200 miles west of Paul's home in Tarsus.

Fresh on their minds was the joy and victory of the governor's conversion in Paphos. Now they found themselves in a new land. Everyone spoke Greek, but they must have encountered some issues. There is no mention of preaching in Perga. They argued.

The missionaries had been traveling for weeks, but something bothered John Mark. Maybe it was the danger. Maybe he did not get along with Paul. Maybe he missed his loved ones back home.

For whatever reason, John Mark had had enough. The port near Perga had ships traveling west toward Rome and east toward Syria and Israel. Mark left the missionaries and caught a ride home.

Not everyone is a missionary or preacher all their life. Mark abandoned Paul and Barnabas. The young man's lack of commitment infuriated Paul.

Mark went back to his friend Peter. At this time, he did the necessary research that he used to write his Gospel of according to Mark at a later date.

Bible verse:

Acts 13:13, "From Paphos, Paul and his companions sailed to Perga in Pamphylia, where John left them to return to Jerusalem."

Discussion question:

Why do you suppose Paul was upset that Mark had left them on this missionary journey?

Prayer Concerns

Week Four – First Journey

Day 22: Went to Antioch in Pisidia

Day 23: Shook dust off at Iconium

Day 24: Stoned and left at Lystra

Day 25: Preached in Derbe and left

Day 26: Appointed church leaders

Day 27: Reported back to Antioch

Day 28: Went to Jerusalem Council

Day 22: Went to Antioch in Pisidia

Hills with cliffs surrounded Pamphylia and Perga. The missionaries left heading north in the spring or summer of AD 48. They climbed past pine trees, then cedar trees, and then no trees at all. Snow had melted in the rugged mountain passes.

Antioch in Pisidia set on a plateau 100 miles north of Perga and west of the Taurus Mountains. Dreary villages with flat-roofed huts and cattle-sheds were scattered amongst an encampment of tents.

Paul and Barnabas found a synagogue in Antioch where they could speak of the Scriptures and faith in God. The same few people spoke most weeks. Here Paul was a guest speaker. He recounted the history of the Jews. Paul spoke of Saul and David. From David came Jesus, their Messiah, and Savior.

They asked him to return and tell them more on the next Sabbath. Excitement built. Crowds gathered. The Jews saw this and got their influential women and prominent men to threaten the missionaries.

The Jews rejected Paul and Barnabas, so they said that God was sending them to the Gentiles. Then the Jews drove the missionaries out of town. Paul and Barnabas shook the dust off their feet and left.

Bible verse:

Acts 13:46, Then Paul and Barnabas answered them boldly: "We had to speak the word of God to you first. Since you reject it and do not consider yourselves worthy of eternal life, we now turn to the Gentiles.

Discussion question:

When might you know that it is time to give up on one ministry so that you can focus on another?

Day 23: Shook dust off at Iconium

Paul and Barnabas departed from Antioch with joy in their hearts that the Holy Spirit allowed them to be persecuted for the sake of the gospel of Christ.

They traveled 100 miles east through the mountain passes along the valley to the large city of Iconium (modern day Konia). This major intersection along the Roman Road lay between Galatia to the north, Pamphylia to the west, and Cilicia to the east.

Again, Paul and Barnabas went to the synagogue. Traditionally, someone would first read the Law in Hebrew. Then people were invited to speak about God in their own language. The missionaries gave a compelling testimony of faith in Jesus Christ. As a result, many Jews and Greeks became Christians.

The non-believing Jews attacked them, and the city was divided, some supporting and some opposing. The two missionaries stayed there several weeks. The Lord allowed them to perform miracles.

Finally, opposition grew to an extreme intensity. When insults and threats of physical abuse failed to stop their preaching, the Gentile and Jewish rulers attempted to stone them to death. Paul and Barnabas escaped and went to Lystra and Derbe.

Bible verse:

Acts 14:11, When the crowd saw what Paul had done, they shouted in the Lycaonian language, "The gods have come down to us in human form!"

Discussion question:

What impact do you expect the miracles Paul did had on those people who witnessed them?

Day 24: Stoned and left at Lystra

Paul grew up southeast of the Taurus Mountains. The neighboring cities of Lystra and Derbe lay at the foot of the other side of these tall mountains. These towns of Lycaonia were 30 miles southeast of Iconium, close enough for regular travel.

Paul and Barnabas came to Lystra and preached the gospel to anyone who would listen. They found a man who was interested in their message of faith in Jesus. This man had never been able to walk. All eyes were on the missionaries. Paul ordered the man to get up. People turned to see what would happen. Then the man leaped up and walked.

The crowds excitedly exclaimed that Barnabas and Paul were the gods Zeus and Hermes. The priest of Zeus prepared to sacrifice of a bull in their honor. Paul and Barnabas insisted that they were all just men who needed Jesus. The commotion led others from Antioch and Iconium to rile up the people.

They stoned Paul until they presumed he was dead. They dragged him out of town, and the disciples surrounded him for protection. Possibly there in the crowd was the young man Timothy, his mother Eunice, or his grandmother Lois. Paul got up and came back into the city. The next day he left town.

Bible verse:

Acts 14:19, "Then some Jews came from Antioch and Iconium and won the crowd over. They stoned Paul and dragged him outside the city, thinking he was dead."

Discussion question:

If you were a disciple from Lystra and you saw them stoning Paul, what concerns might you have?

Day 25: Preached in Derbe and left

As mentioned before, in Lystra, a seed of faith had been planted in the life of the older woman Lois and the younger woman Eunice to follow Christ. They raised up young Timothy in the ways of the Lord and Holy Scripture.

Jesus told his disciples that when they persecute in one town, flee to another. That is what Barnabas and Paul did. They left Lystra and went to Derbe. This town was located near the Black Mountain near the southern end of the Taurus range.

Here in Derbe, the missionaries had a fruitful ministry. They preached the gospel. As a result, many people became disciples of the Lord Jesus Christ. What a joy it is to see a group of people hear the word intently, take it to heart, and then choose to follow God faithfully.

New converts are eager to share their faith with those in their circle of friends and family. One can assume that influence extended back and forth between the small towns of Derbe back to Lystra.

Paul and Barnabas had gone as far as they could go in a circle. They could pass through the Gates of Cilicia to Tarsus. Instead, they had a better idea.

Bible verse:

Acts 14:21 "They preached the gospel in that city and won a large number of disciples. Then they returned to Lystra, Iconium, and Antioch."

Discussion question:

Why do you suppose Paul and Barnabas retraced their steps going back through the same towns?

Day 26: Appointed church leaders

Paul and Barnabas met many new friends and led several to faith in Christ during this missionary journey. However, they had been forced to depart most towns rather quickly. They wanted to help the local churches establish elders in the face of possible persecution.

Therefore the two missionaries retraced their steps. This time the emphasis was on strengthening those who had already believed in a less public manner.

In each town, they gathered with the local church. Paul and Barnabas prayed and fasted as they made their choices. They trained disciples and appointed elders to positions of leadership.

Thus they returned to Lystra where Paul had been previously stoned. From there, they traveled to the big city of Iconium. Gradually they worked their way back to renew their fellowship with Antioch in Pisidia. From there they went south through Pisidia toward the Mediterranean Sea.

They stopped at the inland town of Perga in the region of Pamphylia. Then they traveled a few miles to the coastal city of Attalia (modern day Antalya). From there, they sailed back to Antioch.

Bible verse:

Acts 14:23 "Paul and Barnabas appointed elders for them in each church and, with prayer and fasting, committed them to the Lord, in whom they had put their trust."

Discussion question:

What qualities do you think Paul and Barnabas looked for in the elders that they appointed?

Day 27: Reported back to Antioch

The missionaries who had been commissioned in Antioch returned to their mother church in late AD 48. The church had been praying for them for the better part of the year. Now they were eager to hear what God has done through their ministry.

One can imagine that they held an early missions conference to describe their adventures. They could relate how their ministry in Cyprus had begun with a man named Paulus. Since then the apostle Saul became known as the apostle Paul.

They would recall that three men went out from their church while only two of them returned. Maybe Paul or Barnabas explained about the departure of John Mark.

The missionaries said that they had traveled to yet another Antioch, the one in Pisidia, which was rougher and less cultured. The area populated by the Celtic people of Galatia. They went on to the city of Iconium and then to Lystra where Paul had been stoned and left for dead. Finally, they went to Derbe, preached the gospel, and returned the way they had come. All along the way, many believed in Jesus Christ and became Christians.

Bible verse:

Acts 14:27, "On arriving there, they gathered the church together and reported all that God had done through them and how he had opened a door of faith to the Gentiles."

Discussion question:

What things do you find interesting when you hear missionaries speak in church?

Day 28: Went to Jerusalem Council

The missionaries remained in Antioch most likely until early AD 49. By now Paul and Barnabas were accustomed to doing ministry among the Gentiles. But the Jewish church in Jerusalem thought that all Christians should be circumcised. So the question arose as to whether or not Gentile believers must be circumcised? Paul and Barnabas believed that they should not because they were not Jewish. So they traveled to Jerusalem to discuss the situation.

Paul and Barnabas passed through Phoenicia and Samaria on their way to Jerusalem. They preached the gospel as they went and encouraged believers.

In Jerusalem, they met with Peter and James who was the head of the church. Barnabas and Paul described how God blessed their ministry. James gave instructions about what to do. The Gentiles did not need to be circumcised. James sent them back with a letter of recommendation. Gentiles should not find it difficult to come to Christ.

They were to abstain from food offered to idols and from sexual immorality. These things Paul and Barnabas were already teaching. The Jerusalem church sent Judas and Silas along with them back to Antioch with written instructions from James.

Bible verse:

Acts 15:12, "The whole assembly became silent as they listened to Barnabas and Paul telling about the signs and wonders God had done among the Gentiles through them."

Discussion question:

What amazes you when you hear about miracles done on the mission field?

Prayer Concerns

Week Five – Second Journey

Day 29: Split with Barnabas

Day 30: Took Silas through Cilicia

Day 31: Had Macedonian vision

Day 32: Imprisoned at Philippi

Day 33: Thessalonica and Berea

Day 34: Saw Unknown God Altar

Day 35: Corinth and Ephesus

Day 29: Split with Barnabas

They settled the circumcision controversy. Paul and Barnabas returned to Antioch with Judas and Silas. They described their journey and the discussion they had with the church at Jerusalem.

They shared the instructions from James. They did not require Gentiles to be circumcised. They were to leave behind old idol practices and avoid sexual immorality. Judas returned to Jerusalem, but Silas remained in Antioch available for ministry.

Paul and Barnabas were passionate about their mission. They desired to continue the rapid spread of the gospel among the Gentiles. By the spring of AD 49, they decided to go on another missionary journey. But a new problem arose.

Barnabas wanted to give Mark a second chance. Paul did not trust Mark. He refused to take the man who abandoned him. After a heated argument, Barnabas took Mark. The two set off to their home area of Cyprus to expand on their previous work.

Paul took off on his second missionary journey with Silas. His Roman name was Silvanus. Silas may have been new to missionary travel, but the church in Jerusalem thought him trustworthy.

Bible verse:

Acts 15:39, "They had such a sharp disagreement that they parted company. Barnabas took Mark and sailed for Cyprus."

Discussion question:

When Satan causes a division between Christians, how might God use it to further His purposes?

Day 30: Took Silas through Cilicia

Paul did not follow Barnabas and Mark downriver to Seleucia. The disagreement with Barnabas was so sharp that Paul left by land with Silas. They followed the Roman highway, an eight-foot to a ten-foot wide flat stone road through the hills.

This path took Paul back to his hometown on the way to the cities in Asia Minor. These cities Paul had visited with Barnabas on the previous journey.

Paul and Silas went north from Syria and west through the region of Cilicia. They would have stopped in Paul's hometown of Tarsus. Then they traveled up the Taurus Mountains through the pass of the Cilician Gates. It was the most accessible path through these two-mile-high mountains. They descended the north side and came to Derbe.

Timothy joined their missionary team at Lystra. Paul wanted him because this young man had an excellent reputation. Timothy's father was Greek, but his mother was Jewish. Because of the Jews in that area, Paul had Timothy circumcised.

They traveled for months strengthening believers. Paul wanted to go north from Galatia to Bithynia, but God would not allow it. So they headed west.

Bible verse:

Acts 15:41, "He went through Syria and Cilicia, strengthening the churches."

Discussion question:

Why do you think Gentile churches would be stronger if they followed the instructions Paul received from the Jerusalem church?

Day 31: Had Macedonian vision

The missionaries visited many Gentile churches to pass on the instructions from the Jerusalem church as to how they should conduct their lives.

Dr. Luke had joined their team along the way. By late AD 50 or early AD 51, they reached Troas on the Aegean Sea. Now it was decision time.

They couldn't walk any further west. Paul gazed across the water and prayed. One possibility was to sail south past Ephesus to the Mediterranean Sea, then navigate around Cyprus back to Antioch.

But then Paul had a vision during the night. A man from Macedonia, the region to the north, asked Paul to come over and help. Paul took this as a message from God. The team made plans to go.

The region of Macedonia stretched across the northern edge of the Aegean Sea with Asia Minor to the east and the country of Greece to the west. They sailed to Samothrace, went to Neapolis, and arrived at the Roman military colony of Philippi.

On the Sabbath day, the missionaries went to the river to find a place to pray. They met a merchant woman named Lydia. When she believed their testimony, they baptized her and her household. She insisted that the missionaries stay in her home.

Bible verse:

Acts 16:9, "During the night Paul had a vision of a man of Macedonia standing and begging him, "Come over to Macedonia and help us."

Discussion question:

How do you think Paul was able to determine that the Macedonian vision was from God?

Day 32: Imprisoned at Philippi

On another occasion, they met a female slave who had a spirit that shouted that these missionaries served the Highest God. Paul became fed up, so he commanded the spirit to leave her. And it left her.

Her owners were furious. They told the magistrates that Paul and Silas had stirred up cities against the Roman customs. These magistrates publicly beat them and imprisoned them. The guard put them in the inner cell and fastened their feet in stocks. Paul and Silas prayed and sang hymns to God all night.

About midnight a violent earthquake shook open the cell doors. The guard threatened to kill himself. Paul and Silas shouted for him not to hurt himself because they were all there. Then the jailer came in and asked, "What must I do to be saved?"

They told him to believe on the Lord Jesus Christ, and he and his household would be saved. They all believed. Then the jailer brought Paul and Silas to his home, fed them, and they baptized his family.

In the morning the magistrate told the jailer to release the prisoners. But Paul said that they were Roman citizens, and they had been treated poorly. If they want to release us, they need to come and do it personally. The magistrates were alarmed. Then they released the prisoners Paul and Silas.

Bible verse:

Acts 16:30, "He then brought them out and asked, 'Sirs, what must I do to be saved?'"

Discussion question:

What does the word "saved" mean to you in the context of faith in Jesus Christ?

Day 33: Thessalonica and Berea

Paul traveled to the merchant port of Thessalonica where there was a large Jewish community. Paul preached three weeks in the synagogue that Jesus is the Messiah. Many Jews and Greeks believed in Christ as well as several prominent women.

Other Jews stirred up the crowd telling the officials that these men considered Jesus to be the real King instead of Caesar. When they couldn't find Paul and Silas, they arrested Jason who had protected the missionaries. When it was night, the believers asked Paul and Silas to depart and sent them away.

Berea was a city of beautiful waters at the foot of a mountain range. Jews in the synagogue were of noble character because they studied the Word of God daily. These Bereans eagerly received the gospel of Christ and examined the Scriptures daily to make sure that what was said was true. Many women and men believed in Christ in Berea.

Jews from Thessalonica came, and once again they agitated the crowds and chased them out of town. Paul went to Athens and left instructions for Silas and Timothy to join him as soon as possible. But for a time Silas and Timothy stayed behind to teach the Scriptures in the Berean church.

Bible verse:

Acts 17:11, "Now the Berean Jews were of more noble character than those in Thessalonica, for they received the message with great eagerness and examined the Scriptures every day to see if what Paul said was true."

Discussion question:

What are the advantages of personal Bible study over only learning while at church?

Day 34: Saw Unknown God Altar

While waiting for Silas and Timothy, Paul toured the impressive city of Athens. This free Greek city was 400 years past its prime, while the fame and culture reminded Paul of his classical education.

Athens was full of statues and idols dedicated to every imaginable god. Paul noticed that one was devoted to an unknown god. Thus he stood in the center of the Areopagus and acknowledged to the crowd that they worshiped many gods.

He proceeded to tell them about the true God who created heaven and earth. That true God doesn't live in shrines constructed of wood or stone. The God who created everything made himself known in the person of Jesus Christ. He died to pay for sins and rose from the dead. The Lord commands people all over the world to repent. Some scoffed at Paul's message while others believed.

Many said they wanted to hear Paul preach again. Among those who believed his message was a judge of the Areopagus named Dionysius and a woman named Damaris. Then Paul left Athens. Later he rejoined Silas and Timothy in Corinth.

Bible verse:

Paul traveled to Athens and said in Acts 17:23, "For as I walked around and looked carefully at your objects of worship, I even found an altar with this inscription: to an unknown god. So you are ignorant of the very thing you worship—and this is what I am going to proclaim to you."

Discussion question:

When a Christian shares the gospel, why mention other gods or viewpoints in which people believe?

Day 35: Corinth and Ephesus

When he arrived in the Roman Colony of Corinth, Paul needed to support himself. He joined up with a tent-making couple. Aquila was from Pontus near the Black Sea. He and his wife Priscilla had lived in Italy until Emperor Claudius kicked out all the Jews. They came to believe in Jesus although they still worshiped in the synagogue.

After Silas and Timothy rejoined him in Corinth, Paul devoted himself to full-time ministry. Here he wrote a letter to the Galatians and two letters to the Thessalonians. When the Jews opposed his efforts, Paul said that he would focus on the Gentiles.

God appeared to Paul in a dream to encourage him because there were many Christians in that area. Paul stayed there for a year and a half. Some angry Jews forcibly brought Paul before Gallio, the proconsul of Acadia. They charged him with teaching contrary to the law. Paul left Corinth.

He sailed to Ephesus and ministered there in the synagogue. Many wanted him to stay longer, but Paul had to go home. He promised to return if it was the Lord's will. Paul traveled from Ephesus to Jerusalem and back to the church at Antioch.

Bible verse:

Acts 18:21, "But as he left, he promised, 'I will come back if it is God's will.' Then he set sail from Ephesus."

Discussion question:

Why do you think Paul was able to do ministry full-time after Silas and Timothy arrived?

Prayer Concerns

Week Six – Third Journey

Day 36: Traveled through Galatia

Day 37: Ministry back in Ephesus

Day 38: Encouraged Macedonians

Day 39: Talked on and on at Troas

Day 40: Bid farewell to Ephesians

Day 41: Sought disciples at Tyre

Day 42: Heard Agabus prophecy

Day 36: Traveled through Galatia

Paul made it back to his home church in Antioch for the last time in AD 53. Silas, Timothy, and Dr. Luke were most likely with him. They renewed old friendships and made new ones. The missionaries told the church about their adventures and what God had done throughout their second journey.

The team got needed rest and refreshment before it was time to begin a new mission. Paul set out on his third journey with prayers and encouragement.

They traveled through many towns of Asia Minor. These may have included Tarsus, Derbe, Lystra, Iconium, Pamphylia, and Antioch of Pisidia.

Paul wanted to be in touch with as many churches and believers as possible. He retraced his tracks and sought out new locations.

For example, they visited the cities of Laodicea and Colossae. It was here Paul found himself in the good graces of a noteworthy man called Philemon.

They encouraged the disciples to follow the Lord Jesus Christ faithfully. Paul provided guidance to the pastors and elders. He examined their doctrine and corrected any errors that he discovered. All the while, Paul set his sights on his return to Ephesus.

Bible verse:

Acts 18:23, "After spending some time in Antioch, Paul set out from there and traveled from place to place throughout the region of Galatia and Phrygia, strengthening all the disciples."

Discussion question:

How might you encourage someone whom you will probably never see again?

Day 37: Ministry back in Ephesus

While Paul was gone, an eloquent speaker named Apollos preached powerful messages with flawed doctrine. After Priscilla and Aquila corrected him, they sent Apollos from Ephesus to Corinth.

Finally, Paul's missionary team arrived at Ephesus. Paul had hoped to return. Now he was back. Paul found a dozen disciples who knew only about John's baptism. Paul instructed them in the Holy Spirit and baptized them in the name of Jesus.

Paul preached in the synagogue for three months until he met significant resistance. Then he moved to the hall of Tyrannus for daily lectures. Paul stayed in Ephesus for about two years. He wrote two letters to the Corinthians where he mentioned Apollos; he wrote another letter to the Romans.

The gospel spread because of the strategic location of Ephesus. While God did miracles through Paul, opposition to Christianity continued to rise. One day there was a riot in Ephesus. Those who earned money from the Temple of Artemis worked up the crowds. Paul wanted to get up and speak, but the disciples would not let him. After the trouble died down Paul decided to visit churches in Macedonia and Greece before going to Jerusalem.

Bible verse:

Acts 18:26, "When Priscilla and Aquila heard him [Apollos], they invited him to their home and explained to him the way of God more adequately."

Discussion question:

How does one tell if a preacher is teaching correct Christian doctrine or something that is wrong?

Day 38: Encouraged Macedonians

By AD 56, Emperor Claudius had been poisoned by his wife and replaced by Emperor Nero. The church in Jerusalem was struggling financially. The mother church had fallen on hard times.

One of Paul's goals was to raise money to help the mother church in Jerusalem. There was safety in numbers. Paul traveled with a large group that he had picked up from many churches.

Paul and his team headed back to Macedonia after three years away. The most generous church in that area was the one at Philippi. That church helped Paul out financially on several occasions.

Then Paul went to Greece to collect offerings for Jerusalem and encouraged the believers. Maybe he visited the churches in Thessalonica or Berea. We know Paul returned to Achaia and spent time with the Corinthians.

Having traveled to Greece by going up around the Aegean Sea via Macedonia, Paul now planned to sail directly from Greece to Jerusalem. However, the Jews plotted to capture Paul at the port. When he learned of this, he traveled through Macedonia. He planned to sail to Jerusalem from Asia Minor.

Bible verse:

Acts 20:2, "He traveled through that area, speaking many words of encouragement to the people, and finally arrived in Greece."

Discussion question:

Why do you think so many people traveled with Paul on this missionary journey?

Day 39: Talked on and on at Troas

When they were ready to cross over to Troas, some disciples made the journey by land. Paul sailed around the islands and got there after five days.

The disciples at Troas knew Paul well. Since they rarely saw Paul, they wanted to hear him tell what God had been doing through his ministry. He doubtless encouraged them in their faith.

Paul stayed there a week so he could worship on the Sabbath with them. On Sunday they had one last meeting. They eagerly let him talk as long as he could. So Paul talked on and on until midnight.

One young man named Eutychus listened while Paul was talking on the third floor of the building. When the young man fell asleep, he fell out the window and landed on the ground dead. Everyone feared the worst. But when Paul embraced the man, he came back to life.

Then Paul returned to the meeting. They broke bread together. Paul talked until daylight. Then the meeting ended. The people took Eutychus home.

The missionary team took the ship and sailed to Assos. Paul walked the 30 miles, presumably with some local believers. He arrived the second day.

Bible verse:

Acts 20:9, "Seated in a window was a young man named Eutychus, who was sinking into a deep sleep as Paul talked on and on. When he was sound asleep, he fell to the ground from the third story and was picked up dead."

Discussion question:

Describe a memorable situation where you (or someone you know) fell asleep during church.

Day 40: Bid farewell to Ephesians

Paul sailed to Miletus. There he sent for the elders of the church at Ephesus. He did not want to take time to visit the city because he was in a hurry to reach Jerusalem for the Feast of Pentecost. Paul reminded them of his longtime personal ministry.

He said to them that he knew hardships and prison awaited him. Paul told them that he did not expect to see any of them again. Paul insisted that he was innocent of the blood of all of them because he preached faithfully.

He reminded them that through hard work he supplied for his needs by his own hands. When Paul finished, they wept when they realized that they would never see his face again.

Paul made his way to the ship. Many from the church walked with Paul all the way until he reached the boat. Then they prayed.

Bible verse:

Acts 20:35, "In everything I did, I showed you that by this kind of hard work we must help the weak, remembering the words the Lord Jesus himself said: 'It is more blessed to give than to receive.'"

Discussion question:

Why do you think Paul reminded them that he had supplied his needs with his own hands?

Day 41: Sought disciples at Tyre

They sailed south from Miletus and stopped at the island of Rhodes. When they sailed back over the mainland, they reached the port of Patera.

They found another ship headed to Phoenicia, the land that is the modern-day country of Lebanon and just to the north of Israel.

They sailed south of the island of Cyprus in the opposite direction in which they sailed on their first missionary journey. Then they headed east toward Palestine.

They arrived at Tyre in Phoenicia and unloaded the ship's cargo. The missionaries disembarked and searched for local Christians in that area.

Paul stayed with them for seven days. When the Spirit revealed to the disciples the danger Paul was in, they urged Paul not to go up to Jerusalem.

When it was time for Paul to sail further south, all the believers in that area along with their whole families went to see Paul off on his journey.

Paul sailed from Tyre to Ptolemais and stayed with more Christian brothers and sisters for a day. Then it was on to the port city of Caesarea.

Bible verse:

Acts 21:3, "We sought out the disciples there and stayed with them seven days. Through the Spirit they urged Paul not to go on to Jerusalem."

Discussion question:

Why do you think the disciples in Tyre urged Paul not to go up to Jerusalem?

Day 42: Heard Agabus prophecy

They arrived at the port of Caesarea. There Paul reacquainted himself with Philip the evangelist, one of the original seven deacons with Stephen who was stoned to death with Paul cheering it on. The same Philip who led the Ethiopian eunuch to Christ had become a friend and supporter of Paul, the apostle. Philip had four unmarried daughters who joined in the ministry as they prophesied.

News of Paul's arrival had spread to Jerusalem. After many days, a prophet named Agabus came down the hills to find Paul at the seaside port. The prophet joined Paul and the group around him. He took off Paul's belt. Agabus tied his own hands and feet with the belt. Then he prophesied that the Jews in Jerusalem would do this to Paul. Then the apostle would be handed over to the Gentiles.

Those with Paul feared for his safety. They begged him not to go up to Jerusalem. Paul asked them to stop crying. They were breaking his heart. Then he assured them that he was ready for this and ready to even die for the cause of the Lord Jesus. After this, they started on our way up to Jerusalem. When Paul got to Jerusalem he stayed at the home of Mnason, an early disciple from Cyprus.

Bible verse:

Acts 21:11, "Coming over to us, he took Paul's belt, tied his own hands and feet with it and said, "The Holy Spirit says, 'In this way the Jewish leaders in Jerusalem will bind the owner of this belt and will hand him over to the Gentiles.'"

Discussion question:

How does a missionary handle the risk of leaving loved ones to minister in a dangerous situation?

Prayer Concerns

Week Seven – Final Years

Day 43: Stated Roman citizenship

Day 44: Spoke before Sanhedrin

Day 45: Plot to ambush Paul

Day 46: Appealed to Caesar

Day 47: Preached to Agrippa

Day 48: Shipwrecked on Malta

Day 49: Preached under guard

Day 50: Epilogue and Death

Day 43: Stated Roman citizenship

Paul and his companions arrived in Jerusalem by AD 57. The believers welcomed him. The next day they visited James and the elders at the Jerusalem church. Paul gave them the offering and reported how they had followed James' instructions. The following day as instructed Paul took four men to the temple to meet the Jewish purification rites. This act would prove to the Jews in Jerusalem that Paul was living according to the law. Later Jews from Ephesus saw Paul at the temple and accused Paul of teaching people not to follow the law. They beat Paul until the Romans rescued him. The commander ordered Paul to be bound in chains. He permitted Paul to speak to the crowd. Paul spoke in Aramaic, and they listened.

Paul said he was a Jew, born in Tarsus of Cilicia, but he studied under Gamaliel in Jerusalem. He used to work for the high priest and the Sanhedrin. Then Paul shared his conversion testimony. When he said that the Lord sent him to the Gentiles, the crowd erupted. The soldiers brought Paul to safety. When the commander was about to flog him, Paul told the centurion that he was a Roman citizen. He brought Paul to the commander who then became alarmed that he had put a Roman citizen in chains.

Bible verse:

Acts 22:25, "As they stretched him out to flog him, Paul said to the centurion standing there, 'Is it legal for you to flog a Roman citizen who hasn't even been found guilty?'"

Discussion question:

How might someone use their own citizenship to an advantage in their ministry?

Day 44: Spoke before Sanhedrin

The commander wanted to know why the Jews were accusing Paul. He ordered the chief priests and the Sanhedrin to assemble. Then the commander brought in Paul to speak to them.

Paul explained that he followed God with a good conscience. Ananias ordered Paul to be struck on the mouth, and so Paul yelled at him. They chided Paul for insulting the high priest. Paul apologized. He did not know that Ananias was the high priest.

Then Paul played off their rivalries by saying that he was one of the Pharisees and not the Sadducees. Thus Paul believed in the resurrection of the dead. The Sadducees did not believe in the spirit world, angels, or life after death. The Pharisees believed in all these things. So the Sanhedrin was divided.

The Pharisees thought Paul sounded sensible. The Sadducees wanted to kill him. Violence broke out. The commander feared for Paul's safety, so he had his troops forcefully remove him and take him to the barracks until some decision could be made.

The next night the Lord appeared to Paul and said, "Take courage! As you have testified about me in Jerusalem, so you must also testify in Rome."

Bible verse:

Acts 23:6, "Then Paul, knowing that some of them were Sadducees and the others Pharisees, called out in the Sanhedrin, 'My brothers, I am a Pharisee, descended from Pharisees. I stand on trial because of the hope of the resurrection of the dead.'"

Discussion question:

Why do you think Paul thought it wise to declare that he was a Pharisee?

Day 45: Plot to ambush Paul

The son of Paul's sister heard that some Jews were planning to ambush and kill Paul when they moved him to a new location. The young man entered the barracks and told his uncle. Paul told a centurion to take his nephew to the commander.

The commander asked him what was going on. Paul's nephew told him. The commander warned Paul's nephew not to tell anyone about this.

Then the commander ordered two centurions to get a large detachment of armed soldiers. They were to leave and take Paul by horseback and turn him over safely to Governor Felix in Caesarea. The commander sent along a letter of explanation. The cavalry delivered Paul and the letter. Governor Felix decided that he would put Paul on trial and judge the situation after his accusers had arrived.

Five days later they presented their case against the apostle. Then it was Paul's turn to speak. He said that he had only come to Jerusalem 12 days ago. He had been away for several years but came this time to bring a gift for the poor. His problem was due to Jews from Asia because he believed in the resurrection from the dead. Felix talked with Paul hoping to receive a bribe for his release.

Bible verse:

Acts 23:16, "But when the son of Paul's sister heard of this plot, he went into the barracks and told Paul."

Discussion question:

Describe a time when someone in your family helped you avoid a serious problem.

Day 46: Appealed to Caesar

Festus replaced Governor Felix by AD 59. When the governor visited Jerusalem, the Jewish leaders asked if he would transfer Paul there. They hoped to kill Paul along the way. But the governor said he would see Paul in Caesarea. If they wanted to accuse him, they could do so at Caesarea.

The governor stayed in Jerusalem for more than a week. Then Festus went down to his headquarters in Caesarea. The Jews came to present charges. The governor convened a court to put Paul on trial.

They brought Paul in to hear the severe charges against him. Paul defended himself by saying that he had done nothing wrong, not against the Jewish law nor the temple or Caesar.

Festus asked if he would be willing to stand trial in Jerusalem. Paul knew that would be dangerous. If they didn't kill him along the way, he'd be facing more of a biased Jewish court than a Roman one.

Paul answered that his trial should be in Caesar's court where he already was. He was willing to die, but he had done nothing deserving death. Sensing this was his last chance, Paul appealed to Caesar! Thus Festus declared. "To Caesar, you will go!"

Bible verse:

Acts 25:11, "If, however, I am guilty of doing anything deserving death, I do not refuse to die. But if the charges brought against me by these Jews are not true, no one has the right to hand me over to them. I appeal to Caesar!"

Discussion question:

In what ways do you think God had kept Paul safe throughout his legal trials?

Day 47: Preached to Agrippa

A few days after Paul appealed to Caesar, King Agrippa and Bernice arrived at Caesarea to pay their respects to the new Governor Festus. Paul's case came up in conversation. The governor told them that it was a religious dispute. So he ordered Paul to be held until he could send him to Caesar.

Agrippa was familiar with the Jewish faith and the stories about Jesus. He told Festus that he wanted to hear Paul for himself. Plans were made.

The hall was filled with prominent men and with military officers. Agrippa and Bernice came in with a regal ceremony. Finally, Governor Festus brought in Paul and introduced him. Festus said that he found no reason to put him to death. But he needed to write something to Caesar about Paul.

So Paul made his defense to King Agrippa. Paul said that he lived all his life as a strict Pharisee. Then Paul gave his testimony. He urged Agrippa to believe in Jesus as he believed in the prophets. Agrippa asked him if he thought he could persuade him to be a Christian so quickly. Paul hoped the king would believe, no matter how long it takes. Agrippa said to Festus, "This man could have been set free if he had not appealed to Caesar."

Bible verse:

We read in Acts 26:28 that "Agrippa said to Paul, 'Do you think that in such a short time you can persuade me to be a Christian?'"

Discussion question:

If you have been persuaded to become a Christian, how long did that process take?

Day 48: Shipwrecked on Malta

Paul set sail for Italy along with other prisoners under the care of Julius the centurion. Aristarchus from Thessalonica was with Paul and his friends.

They sailed to Sidon where Julius kindly let Paul get off the ship and visit with friends who provided for his needs. From there they sailed past the east side of Cyprus because of the winds. They reached the coast of Cilicia and headed west to Pamphylia. They landed at Myra in Lycia and changed ships.

They headed out for Italy, but a storm blew them off course to the south side of the island of Crete. Paul advised them to stop, but they ignored him. They were behind schedule and decided to sail on. But then they got caught by hurricane force winds.

For 14 days the ship was battered by the wind and waves of the western Mediterranean Sea. The sun was hidden from view. They threw the cargo and ship tackle into the sea. Paul told them that though the ship will be destroyed, all 276 of them would live. They ran aground on the island of Malta. The centurion kept the soldiers from killing any of the prisoners. They all survived. The islanders kindly built a fire in the rain and cold. A viper grabbed Paul's hand, but he shook it off without any harm.

Bible verse:

Acts 27:43, "But the centurion wanted to spare Paul's life and kept them from carrying out their plan. He ordered those who could swim to jump overboard first and get to land."

Discussion question:

Why do you think that the centurion wanted to spare Paul's life?

Day 49: Preached under guard

They spent three winter months on the island of Malta. Then they boarded a ship headed for Rome. They stopped on Sicily at Syracuse for three days and reached the lower end of Italy at Rhegium. A couple days later favorable winds brought them to Puteoli. Paul spent a week with some Christian brothers and sisters before going on to Rome.

The word spread that Paul was coming along with his ministry friends. Believers came to meet them, some at the Forum of Appius and others at the Three Taverns. Paul thanked God for them, being much encouraged. Paul arrived in Rome in AD 60.

He was allowed to live by himself, with a soldier to guard him. One of the first things Paul did was to invite the local Jewish leaders to hear his story.

He assured them that he had done nothing against the Jews, their law, or their customs. He explained how he felt compelled to appeal to Caesar. The Jews said they had not heard anything bad about him, but they all knew of the Christian sect. They were okay until he preached about Jesus and said that Gentiles could be saved. Paul taught for two years in his own rented house. There he wrote Philemon, Colossians, Ephesians, and Philippians.

Bible verse:

Acts 28:16, "When we got to Rome, Paul was allowed to live by himself, with a soldier to guard him."

Discussion question:

Why do you think Paul was given so much freedom as a prisoner in Rome?

Day 50: Epilogue and Death

Paul's plan in AD 56 was to visit Rome and then Spain. We read in Romans 15:28, "So after I have completed this task and have made sure that they have received this contribution, I will go to Spain and visit you on the way." He did not make it then.

According to tradition, Paul's friend Barnabas was stoned to death on Cyprus at Salamis in AD 61.

It appears Paul was released from prison in AD 62. About that time he wrote the books of 1 Timothy and this in Titus 3:12: "As soon as I send Artemas or Tychicus to you, do your best to come to me at Nicopolis because I have decided to winter there."

There is some historical evidence that Paul visited Spain in AD 63 to continue his missionary work. The Great Fire of Rome burned for six days in July of AD 64. Nero blamed the fire on the Christians, and a great persecution followed.

By AD 64 Paul wrote in 2 Timothy 4:11, "Only Luke is with me. Get Mark and bring him with you, because he is helpful to me in my ministry."

Around AD 65 Paul was imprisoned in Rome for the second time. Paul was put to death as a martyr for his faith in the year AD 66.

Bible verse:

2 Timothy 4:7, "I have fought the good fight, I have finished the race, I have kept the faith."

Discussion question:

What do you hope people will remember about your faith and your spiritual life?

Prayer Concerns

Leader's Guide

Welcome to small group leadership! Small groups meet for a variety of reasons. Groups need leaders. If you are leading a small group, praise God. You serve a vital function. Consider these questions.

What is the purpose of your group?

Your small group exists for one or more excellent reasons. You benefit when you keep the purpose of your group clearly in mind. I list several options. Pick a primary one or come up with your own.

To lead new people to faith in Christ.

To build fellowship among believers.

To learn how to be a disciple of Jesus.

To enjoy a hobby with fellow believers.

To grow into a future church congregation.

To bring community to those who are alone.

To study the Bible and gain in knowledge.

To meet with others in similar life situations.

To pray for the needs of those you care about.

To provide an opportunity for service projects.

Whom do you expect to be in your group?

Where do your people come from? Are they part of your church congregation? Are they people in a similar life situation? Are they co-workers? Are they the same gender or in the same age bracket? Do they live in the same community?

Does your group already exist? Is your group open to new members? Or is your group full? If you are the leader, you should know. If you are open to new members, how similar do they need to be to those already in your group?

Where do you meet?

People need to know where to find you. Small groups may meet at a church building, in a home, in a restaurant, at a business during breaks, after classes at school, or just about any reasonable place that people can carry on a conversation.

When do you meet?

Make sure your group members know what day you meet and for how long. Do you meet daily? Do you meet weekly? Regular meetings work best.

How do you lead a discussion?

Picture yourself in a meeting. One person does all the talking. Everyone else sits there quietly. Bored. Okay, that's not the goal. We want participation!

You as the leader can encourage your small group by promoting a balanced discussion. A study guide like this one is designed for conversation. Try this. Read the passage aloud. Ask the questions one at a time. Stop talking. Let others in your group talk.

Who reads the passage?

You can. Some people hate to read out loud. If all the people in your group are comfortable reading out loud, then you may take turns. If only some people like to read, you can ask for volunteers. You decide that. Make sure that whoever reads can be heard and understood by others in the group.

Who asks the question?

You can. It is easier for the leader to control the flow of the discussion if you ask the questions. But if you need to break it up, then ask for help. "Can I have a volunteer to read the next question?" or "Would someone read question number 3 for us?"

What if no one will answer the question?

If people know, like, and trust you, they are likely to participate. If they have interest in the subject, they will want to add something to the discussion.

If they feel comfortable in the environment, they are more likely to share. Many people do not like silence. After you ask the question, stop talking. Wait a few moments. Usually, someone will speak.

When is it your turn to answer the question?

If no one else has anything to say, then it is your turn. If you have something useful to add, share it now. When you finish, ask if anyone else has something that they would like to share.

If a question seems very personal or difficult, you may choose to go first to break the ice. When one person answers, it triggers ideas for other people. Be careful. Make sure you do not talk too much.

What if you cannot answer the question?

Then don't answer. You do not need to have all the answers. However, if you read the passage and all the questions in advance (before the meeting), you have more time to think up a good response.

What if someone won't stop talking?

You need talkers to have a conversation. Beware of the person who delivers a lengthy monologue for every question. That's not a discussion.

Talkers will talk. Let them at first. Eventually, they will stop or at least need to breathe! Thank them and ask if anyone else has something to share.

If one person continues to dominate the replies to every question, and if it seems to bother others in your group, you can try this. "Let's let someone else answer this next question first."

How long should you spend on each question?

You and those in your group know, and even feel, how long a meeting should last. Stay on schedule. You need to keep moving on to the next question.

This book is designed to be covered in multiple meetings. Determine how much of the material you plan to include for each meeting.

If you operate on a time limit for the meeting, stop on time. You can add or skip questions. You can pick up next time where you left off this time.

Be a good leader. People will love you for it.

Acknowledgments

The cover is a picture of the Sea of Galilee.
Cover design by **fiverr.com/pro_ebookscovers**.
Dates and timeline for Paul's life came from:
blueletterbible.org/study/paul/timeline.cfm.
Thank you to Julie Sawyer for her editorial help.

About the Author

Tim Sawyer writes on religion, chess, and history. He is a former sports editor, insurance underwriter, pastor, baseball chaplain, and classification officer.

Tim Sawyer books:

Jacob: A flawed man loved by God

Peter: A model for following Jesus

Paul: A missionary for Jesus

Mary: Women with Jesus

Peter, Paul and Mary (Bible study collection)

Painter to Preacher to Prison (Tim's story)

Called: Sherwood Sawyer Church Pastor

Bible Word Search: Large Print Puzzles

amazon.com/author/timsawyer

Made in the USA
Las Vegas, NV
30 October 2023

79941041R00075